AR.4.3 PTS:0.5

CAN YOU FIND IT?

Find It in a
RAIN FOREST

Dee Phillips

GARETH**STEVENS**
GS PUBLISHING
A Member of the WRC Media Family of Companies

Please visit our web site at: **www.garethstevens.com**
For a free color catalog describing Gareth Stevens Publishing's list of high-quality books and multimedia programs, call 1-800-542-2595 (USA) or 1-800-387-3178 (Canada). Gareth Stevens Publishing's fax: (414) 332-3567.

Library of Congress Cataloging-in-Publication Data

Phillips, Dee, 1967-
    Find it in a rain forest / by Dee Phillips.
      p. cm. — (Can you find it?)
    ISBN 0-8368-6299-6 (lib. bdg.)
    1. Rain forest animals—Juvenile literature.   I. Title.
  QL112.P48   2006
  578.734—dc22   2005056346

This North American edition first published in 2006 by
Gareth Stevens Publishing
A Member of the WRC Media Family of Companies
330 West Olive Street, Suite 100
Milwaukee, WI 53212 USA

This U.S. edition copyright © 2006 by Gareth Stevens, Inc. Original edition copyright © 2005 by ticktock Entertainment Ltd. First published in Great Britain in 2005 by ticktock Media Ltd., Unit 2, Orchard Business Centre, North Farm Road, Tunbridge Wells, Kent TN2 3XF.

Gareth Stevens series editor: Dorothy L. Gibbs
Gareth Stevens graphic designer: Charlie Dahl
Gareth Stevens art direction: Tammy West

Picture credits: (t=top, b=bottom, l=left, r=right, c=center)
FLPA: 2, 4-5, 7, 8-9c, 9tr, 10, 14, 17, 23.
Every effort has been made to trace the copyright holders for the pictures used in this book. We apologize in advance for any unintentional omissions and would be pleased to insert the appropriate acknowledgements in any subsequent edition.

Printed in the United States of America

1 2 3 4 5 6 7 8 9 10 09 08 07 06

Words that appear in the glossary are printed in **boldface** type the first time they occur in the text.

Contents

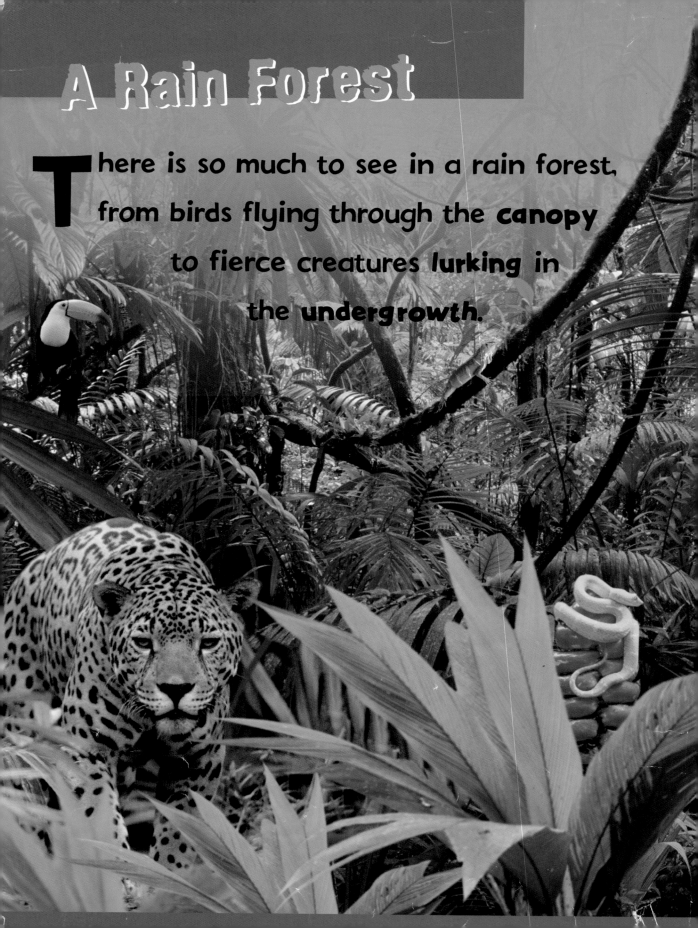

A Rain Forest

There is so much to see in a rain forest, from birds flying through the **canopy** to fierce creatures **lurking** in the **undergrowth**.

What can you find in a rain forest?

Sloth

Toucan

Jaguar

Iguana

Tapir

Parrot

Monkey

Viper

Vines

Sloth

A sloth may be the laziest animal in the world. It moves very, very slowly and spends twenty hours a day sleeping in the rain forest's tall trees.

A sloth stays still for such a long time that green **algae** grows in its hair.

A sloth has three claws on each **limb**. It hooks them around branches to hold on tightly.

When a sloth is active, it moves at a speed of only about 7 feet (2 meters) a minute.

Toucan

Toucans spend most of their time high in the trees. They are one of easiest kinds of birds to identify because of their enormous **bills**. Toucans use their big bills to reach into trees and grab food.

Its bright yellow, black, and red **plumage** helps a toucan recognize other toucans and find a **mate**.

A toucan's bill, or beak, can measure up to 8 inches (20 centimeters) long!

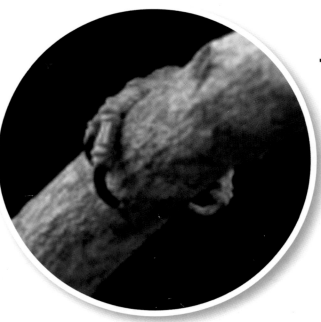

Toucans have strong feet that can wrap around branches to hold on tight.

Jaguar

Jaguars belong to the cat family. Most of these big cats have yellow coats spotted with black rings, but some jaguars are all black, and some jaguars are white.

The patterns on a jaguar's coat help it blend in with its surroundings. Each cat has slightly different markings.

Jaguars live in the wild in Central America, South America, and the southern United States.

A jaguar can swim very well and sometimes catches fish to eat.

Iguana

There are about 650 different kinds of iguanas. Some are very small, but the big ones grow to more than 6 feet (2 m) long.

The skin of a young iguana is very light green. This color helps it hide among the green leaves of the rain forest.

Iguanas are excellent climbers. Their long claws help them grip vines and tree branches.

An iguana spends a lot of time **basking** in the Sun to warm its body.

Tapir

A tapir is an unusual-looking animal. It has a very large head, almost no neck, and its nose looks like a short trunk.

Because tapirs have such poor eyesight, they use their sense of smell to search for food.

When tapirs are frightened, they may dive into water to hide. They are very good swimmers.

Tapirs stay hidden from **predators** during the day. They come out at night to search for food.

A tapir has three toes on its back legs and four toes on its front legs.

Parrot

Parrots are noisy birds with bright plumage and powerful beaks. They live high in the branches of rain forest trees.

A parrot cleans its colorful feathers by carefully pulling them through its beak – one feather at a time.

A parrot has a hook at the end of its beak. It uses the hook to scoop out the soft parts of fruit. It uses its strong lower beak to crack open seeds.

Parrots have strong wings and can fly very fast over short distances.

Monkey

Many different kinds of monkeys live in rain forests. Monkeys are part of the same family as apes and gorillas, but monkeys are smaller and have long tails.

The golden lion tamarin is a very small monkey – about the size of a squirrel. Its bushy golden mane makes it look like a lion.

Like most monkeys, tamarins spend a lot of time high in the trees, jumping or swinging from branch to branch. Their long, thin fingers help them hang on to the branches.

Most monkeys also use their long tails like an extra hand.

Tamarins spend all day in the trees, and at night, they even rest in the trees.

19

Viper

A viper is a **poisonous** snake. Its **fangs** fold up inside its mouth and swing downward when the snake wants to bite something.

The spiny scales over this viper's eyes look like eyelashes. The snake is called an eyelash viper.

A pit between a viper's eyes can sense differences in heat, which helps the snake find its **prey.**

Vipers in the rain forest usually rest during the day and come out at night to hunt. Their favorite foods include small **mammals**, lizards, frogs, and birds.

Vines

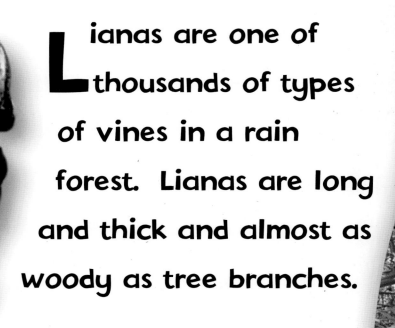

Lianas are one of thousands of types of vines in a rain forest. Lianas are long and thick and almost as woody as tree branches.

Most kinds of vines grow **tendrils**, which wind around trees to provide support.

Some types of vines are called strangler vines. They grow so thick that they can kill the trees supporting them.

As vines spread from one tree to another, they start to look like ropes draped across the rain forest canopy.

Glossary

algae – tiny plants that have no roots, stems, or leaves

basking – lying in the warmth of the Sun

bills – the mouthparts, or beaks, on birds

canopy – the highest treetops in a rain forest

fangs – hollow, pointed teeth used for biting and injecting poison

limb – an arm or a leg

lurking – waiting or hiding in a secret way

mammals – animals with backbones that give birth to live babies and feed their babies milk from the mother's body

mate – the male or female of a pair of animals that come together to produce young, or offspring

plumage – the feathers that cover a bird's body

poisonous – containing a substance that can cause illness or death

predators – animals that hunt and kill other animals for food

prey – an animal that is killed by another animal for food

tendrils – the long curls, or coils, of a plant that can grab on to or wind around something for support

undergrowth – the plants that grow under trees

The Forgotten King

WRITTEN BY

Kenneth Padgett & Shay Gregorie

ILLUSTRATED BY

Stephen Crotts

Wolfbane
BOOKS

KENNETH PADGETT lives in the South Carolina lowcountry with his family. He is a total Bible nerd who often daydreams of cosmic mountains and the Mended Wood.

SHAY GREGORIE also makes his home in the South Carolina lowcountry with his family. He likes to write silly poems to his homeschooling superhero wife to make her smile. They have enough children to fend off an army of dufflepuds.

STEPHEN CROTTS is an illustrator who lives in Rock Hill, South Carolina with his wife and two daughters. He enjoys playing banjo, looking for snakes, and cooking in giant iron pots.

Copyright © 2022 by Wolfbane Books

Published by
Wolfbane Books
1164 Porcher's Bluff Road
Mount Pleasant, SC 29466
www.wolfbanebooks.com

Cover and interior illustrations by Stephen Crotts
Cover and interior design by Brannon McAllister

Hardcover edition ISBN: 978-1-7366106-1-9
First Edition

Printed in China
10 9 8 7 6 5 4 3 2

For Eisley and Lyla — This story has swirled in and around your imaginations for as long as you've lived. May you always carry its truths in your hearts and teach them to your children and grandchildren.

—KENNETH

For Miriam, Esther, Shay, Silas, Lucy, Gabriel, Marigold and Gideon — I'm unworthy to have children as wonderful as you. May you never be too big for this small story.

—SHAY

For Lena Ruth and Della Mercy — "Those who look to him are radiant; their faces are never covered with shame."

—STEPHEN

In the days of old, a long time ago,
There was a high mountain with a village below.
Up on the mountain stood a castle great,
Where the King would gaze down from his big, golden gate.
The people loved the King, and he loved them.
Each day they'd look up, and sing songs to him.

The most loving and joyful,
The best King they'd had.
In good weather he'd visit
The happy and sad.

His kindness spread like warm sun rays,
So that everyone loved much like him in those days.

But, one dark moonless night,
An evil wizard appeared,
Slithering into the village,
With a long scraggly beard.

Where did he come from?
No one really knows.
But, he hated the King
From his head to his toes.

Was he jealous of them? Perhaps he was just rude.
"Why are these people in such a good mood?!
If I were the king, I'd set them all straight!
I'd treat them all badly and teach them to hate!"

"Now here's an idea!
I'll cast a dark spell!"
Then he did it so shrewdly
That no one could tell!

A dark, heavy cloud settled over the town.
When the people woke up, they felt gloomy and down!

All around, it was dreary and gray.
When they looked up, there was no light of day!
And no sight of the castle way up in the sky.

They felt a bit lonely and didn't know why.

Before long, the people forgot their King.
No more getting together to look up and sing.
Now they spent their time bickering, snickering, and mad.
The evil curse turned all the good into bad!

Their hearts grew darker as each day passed.
The King missed them so much! How long would this last?
He sent down many servants through the cloud to bring cheer,
To proclaim that he loved them, that he was still near!

They'd say, "He's still up there just through the cloud!
If you sing he will hear you, so sing really loud!"
But the villagers laughed, "A King up in the sky?!
You're crazy! Go back, and don't tell us that lie!"

The wizard loved what he heard as he lurked.

The King was forgotten! The curse really worked!

Not a soul believed the King's men, not even one.
So the King called for his most loyal servant, his son!
The valiant Prince knew right where to go:
Down through the cloud to the village below!
He rode like the wind, taking turns with great care,
And leapt from his horse when he reached the town square.

He marched straight up the steps and sounded the bell,
And he started to tell them of the evil spell.

"Long ago you loved my father, the King!
He's still on the throne! It's good news I bring!
You have to believe me; he sent me! It's true!
He wants to bring JOY back to all of you!"

The people just grumbled and mumbled and groaned,
And said, "Who are you? Go on back to your home!"

The Prince held his ground and stood firm as a tree.
He reached for his bow, and they started to flee.
"No, wait! The King loves you!" he pleaded, "Don't go!"

Then he cried,

Long Live the King!

As he pulled back his bow.

The long, sharp arrow flew straight through the air.
It ripped through the curse with a thunderous tear!

All silently gazed at the gash in the cloud.
"It is finished," he said in the midst of the crowd.

Everyone heard him, and marveled at the sight.
Just then — on the Prince — a shower of light!

The wizard looked around
And like a roach tried to flee.
But he stumbled on his beard
And smacked his head on a tree!

The cloud had been pierced; it began to fade fast.
The Prince got the wizard! Justice at last!
Locked up in a carriage like an unwanted beast,
Then banished far over the hills to the east.

When the wizard was gone, the cloud went away,
And all could see the great castle that day!

The people honked and hooted and hollered for joy.
Then one voice rang loudly, it was just a small boy.
"The King's coming down with his men on the march!"
And they stopped when the King stood under the arch.

All fell silent when he started to speak.
Not a cough, a sneeze, or even a squeak.
Would the King treat them kindly
Even though he'd been forgotten?
Though they'd bickered, and snickered,
And acted plain rotten?

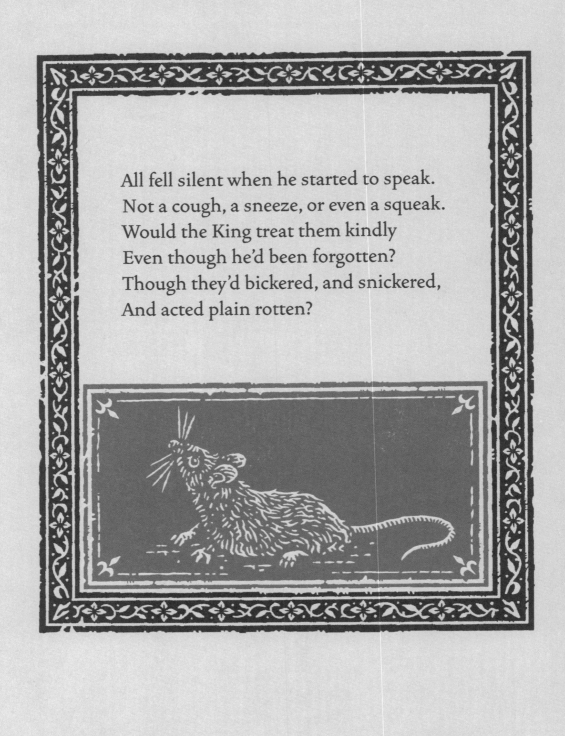

The people just stood there, not knowing what to do.
The King spoke plainly, his voice deep and true:
"The time has come! I am moving for good!"
The people were puzzled. He pointed down where he stood!
What did he mean? Was there a house he could buy?
His castle was still way up there in the sky!

The next thing they saw—
The castle coming apart!
Piece by piece each stone
Was loaded in carts!
Down the mountain they wheeled,
And with festive fanfare,
They put it together
Right in the town square!

"With my castle right here,
I will always protect you.
No evil curse will ever infect you!
Forever and always,
I'll love you. It's true!
To the end of the age,
I'll be right here with you!"

The King did as he said, with the Prince on his right.
They reigned in the village as their castle shone bright.

The people loved again, no more tears, not a one.
All was light, love, and laughter — Hail the King's brave son!

And I heard a loud voice from the throne saying, "Behold, the dwelling place of God is with man. He will dwell with them, and they will be his people, and God himself will be with them as their God. He will wipe away every tear from their eyes, and death shall be no more, neither shall there be mourning, nor crying, nor pain anymore, for the former things have passed away."

—REVELATION 21:3-4